WASHINGTON D.C.

WASHINGTON D.C.

PHOTOGRAPHY
BY ROBERT REYNOLDS

TEXT
BY THOMAS K. WORCESTER

WASHINGTON D.C.

iv

International Standard Book Number 0-912856-08-4
Library of Congress Catalog Card Number 72-78004
Copyright® 1972 by Publisher · Charles H. Belding
2000 N.W. Wilson · Portland, Oregon 97209 · 503-224-7777
Designer · Robert Reynolds
Text · Thomas K. Worcester
Printer · Graphic Arts Center
Binding · Lincoln & Allen
Printed in the United States of America

The statue of freedom by Sculptor Thomas Crawford, towering above the Capitol dome, stands 19½ feet tall and weighs 7½ tons. The figure was erected in 1863. The thirteen fluted columns surmounting the cap represent the first thirteen states.

Painting, glorifying the work of America's first president, George Washington, hangs 180 feet above the floor of the Capitol rotunda. This *Apotheosis of Washington* was executed by Constantino Brumidi. Right: The great white dome of the United States Capitol is a major symbol of the nation, the home of Congress, and a vessel of history. St. Peter's Church in Rome provided the model for the cap of the Capitol dome.

"We have built no national temples but the capitol,
we consult no common oracle but the constitution."

RUFUS CHOATE, member of congress

Chinese ceramic bowl of the Yuan Dynasty, made during the fourteenth century. This museum piece represents one of the approximately ten thousand cataloged items in the Freer Gallery of Art, deeded to the nation by Charles Lang Freer. Right: Interior of Chinese art room. It is considered to be one of the world's most distinguished collections of oriental art. Located on the Mall at Twelfth Street.

The Library of Congress has indeed become a national storehouse of culture and knowledge, serving not only Congress, but the whole of America. Constructed of New Hampshire granite, this ornate renaissance-styled building and its art forms are a treasure for the eye to see. Right: Camera captures unusual bark design of a sycamore tree on the Capitol grounds.

Executive Office Building situated next door to the White House originally housed the State, War and Navy departments. When this massive, rococo structure was built 1871-1887 it was considered the world's largest office building. Right: Bronze figure "Winged Victory" situated atop an 80 foot column south of the Executive Office Building. A memorial to the members of the Army's First Infantry Division who died in World War I and World War II.

Marble statue of General Ulysses S. Grant by
Franklin Simons in the rotunda of the Capitol, a gift
from the Grand Army of the Republic. Right: The
Senate reception room is highlighted by a ceiling
fresco painting by Constantino Brumidi.

TEXT BY THOMAS K. WORCESTER

JENKINS HILL

Jenkins Hill rises to an elevation of about 88 feet above the Potomac River about two miles from the confluence of the Anacostia River and the Potomac in western Maryland. Two hundred years ago, the hill was covered with lush underbrush and woods, and in the immediate surroundings only an occasional rustic home interrupted the virgin nature of the area. Nearby were the cities of Georgetown, Maryland, and Alexandria, Virginia—the centers of commerce and social life in that section of the lower Potomac.

Jenkins Hill today is the site of one of the most significant buildings in the world: the United States Capitol. How it came to be placed there is a story of the remarkable genius of the early men who determined the nature of this country. How it remains is a continuing tribute to those founders and to other gallant men and women who have nurtured the idea that is America.

The hill and its near environs (including Alexandria and Georgetown) are part of a 100-square-mile tract of land selected by President George Washington as the site of a Federal City, the seat of government for the nation. The city was born of compromise, and has lived in contrast and paradox throughout its history.

Perhaps the idea of a Federal City became serious because of an incident in 1783. Continental Army troops seeking back pay marched on Philadelphia where Congress was in session. The members of Congress, fearing harm from the aggrieved soldiers, called on the Philadelphia militia for protection, but the militia refused to act. The aroused soldiers soon encircled the Pennsylvania State House where Congress met, and, with bayonets fixed, demanded their overdue pay. But Congress dismissed the demand. James Madison, alarmed for the safety of the lawmakers, called for an immediate adjournment of Congress, and suggested it was "time to remove to some other place." But Congress remained in session until the usual hour of closure, then recessed for the weekend. On the following Tuesday, Congress retreated to the safety of Princeton, leaving the Philadelphia hall to the soldiers. But the idea of a separate federal territory with a militia to protect the Congress was afloat and members now talked seriously of a location.

The question of a permanent site for the federal government had been raised in Congress as early as 1779. At that time, it seemed likely that the government would be located in some existing city, where there would be ready-made facilities for the legislators and the federal workers. But what city? More than one had been suggested as the ideal location for the government: there was Boston, where the first shot of the Revolutionary War had been fired; and Yorktown, where victory was grasped; and Philadelphia, where independence had been proclaimed. New York, Newport, Williamsburg, Wilmington, Lancaster, Trenton, Annapolis—all sought the honor.

Debate on the location of the national capital lasted until 1790, when the issue appeared hopelessly deadlocked in a North-South standoff. But through the careful political engineering of Thomas Jefferson and Alexander Hamilton, a compromise was reached: in trade for having the national capital situated on the Potomac River, southern Congressmen would support a bill which shifted fiscal responsibility for the state war debts to the federal government. This measure was of particular benefit to the northern states which had had the major share of financing the Revolutionary War. Thus the northern states received needed funds, while the southern states rejoiced at having the capital site nearby. Congress took two further steps in 1790 to settle the establishment of the Federal City: Philadelphia was selected to be the temporary site for ten years, or until the first Monday in December, 1800, when the capital would be moved to its permanent site; and secondly, President Washington was entrusted with choosing "on the river Potomac" a territory, ten miles square, which was to become the federal territory and the permanent seat of the United States Government.

What would be the nature of the Federal City? A residential city for legislators, statesmen, and federal employees? Or a center of commerce for trade with the world's ports? Or a mixture of both? And what of its future?

President Washington had little trouble deciding on the location for he was familiar with the area of the Potomac, having ridden through its forests and over the hills much of his life. He chose the spot where the city now stands for its intrinsic beauty, its location relative to the Potomac, and for its centrality.

Congress also authorized the president to appoint three commissioners to survey the district, under his direction, and to establish title to the land in the name of the federal government. The state of Maryland ceded about 68 square miles to the government and the state of Virginia 32 square miles, thus establishing the federal district. From the very beginning a confusion of names was inherent in the district and the city, for the cities of Georgetown and Alexandria were already in existence, but were included in the new federal district. But the three commissioners appointed by President Washington named the new Federal City "City of Washington," and the area in the state of Maryland, outside the City of Washington and Georgetown, was called the County of Washington. The area in Virginia outside Alexandria was known as the County of Alexandria. Thus in its initial stages, the District of Columbia, so named by the commissioners, included the City of Washington, Georgetown, Alexandria, the County of Alexandria (Virginia) and the County of Washington (Maryland).

For the design of the new Federal City George Washington selected Major Pierre Charles L'Enfant, a French engineer who had served with the American forces during the Revolutionary War. When he learned of the plans for the new city, L'Enfant wrote to President Washington from New York:

"Sir: The late determination of Congress to lay the foundation of a city which is to become the capital of this vast empire offers so great an occasion of acquiring reputation to whoever may be appointed to conduct the execution of the business that your Excel-

lency will not be surprised that my ambition and the desire I have of becoming a useful citizen should lead me to wish a share in the undertaking.

"No nation, perhaps, had ever before the opportunity offered them of deliberately deciding on the spot where the capital city should be fixed . . . And, although the means now within the power of the country are not such as to pursue the design to any great extent, it will obvious that the plan should be drawn on such a scale as to leave room for the aggrandizement and embellishment which the increase of the wealth of the nation will permit it to pursue at any period, however remote. Viewing the matter in this light, I am fully sensible of the extent of the undertaking."

L'Enfant has been described as proud, haughty, intractable, and with an "untoward" temper, but he also was honest, loyal, and extremely gifted. Washington perceived him as a scientific man with considerable taste and professional knowledge, "better qualified than anyone who has come within my knowledge in this country." The President informed L'Enfant to begin work at once.

L'Enfant left New York and went to Georgetown in early March, 1791, where he found the selected site clouded by mist and soaked by heavy rainfall. Eager to begin, L'Enfant rode horseback throughout the area, and though visibility was restricted, he was enthralled by the countryside and the prospects it offered for the city. In his first survey of the area he selected Jenkins Hill as the site of the Capitol, or Federal House as the designer called it. He later wrote:

"I could discover no one (spot) so advantageously to greet the congressional building as is that on the west end of Jenkins heights, which stands as a pedestal waiting for a monument."

L'Enfant's vision of the Federal City was that of an area where the government officials and federal employees would work in the surroundings of monuments and memorials to the famous. His plan called for avenues up to 160 feet wide, frequent circles and squares, diagonal avenues that cut across the city to allow traffic to move from one area to another with ease, and a grand avenue from the "Federal House" to the "President's Palace."

L'Enfant's plan has been said to resemble a wheel, with the Capitol at the hub. The plan is original, though in some ways its major features—open vistas, major arterials from point to point— are similar to the Versailles, where he spent his early years. The broad avenues and circles also were used in Paris, another city with which he was intimately familiar.

The vigor with which L'Enfant pursued the plan eventually led to his dismissal as supervisor of construction of the city. This was after he ordered the destruction of a house belonging to the cousin of one of the District Commissioners, which was being constructed contrary to L'Enfant's plans.

In his later years, Pierre Charles L'Enfant roamed the streets of Washington and haunted the halls of the Capitol, vigorously defending his plan for the Federal City. He died in 1825, and he was buried at the foot of a tree on the Digges property near Washington. His entire estate at that time was valued at $46.00.

The credibility of his plan has captured the imaginations of city planners decades later, though even the brilliant L'Enfant could not envision the congestion that modern automobile traffic would cause in his beloved city.

While some steps were taken to institute the L'Enfant plan during the early years of the capital's life, for the most part Washington remained a backward town, with dirt streets, poor sanitation facilities, and undeveloped land until the 1870's. Then, through a series of circumstances that can only be considered fortuitous to the development of the city, a man was elevated into power in the city who launched Washington on the course that has made it the city it is today. That man was Alexander Robey Shepherd.

In 1871, Congress established a territorial form of government for the District of Columbia, with a governor, an 11-member legislative assembly, and a 22-man house of delegates. President Grant appointed Henry D. Cooke as governor of the district, and Alexander Shepherd was made a chairman of the Board of Public Works. Shepherd, a native of Washington, was an ex-member of the city council and head of a Citizen's Reform Association. He soon became the most powerful man in the territorial government, and with the energy and ambition of a zealot set out to make the city the most beautiful in the world.

Shepherd constructed many miles of sewers, paved the streets, put in sidewalks, moved railroad tracks, established parks, and installed street lights. He also planted trees—hundreds of trees. By 1873 he was made governor of the District, and had nearly total control of the operations of the District. But a financial panic that year, coupled with a Congressional investigation which unearthed a heavy debt for the city, forced Congress to abolish the territorial form of government, and Shepherd's brief reign over the city was over. Not, however, before he had made the improvements give credence to the original plan of L'Enfant. Though castigated at the time, Shepherd proved to be a genuine saviour for the city, and since has been honored as the "Maker of Washington."

L'Enfant's plan withstood the test of scrutiny and comparison once again 100 years later when Congress established a commission to plan for the entire District of Columbia what L'Enfant had done for the Federal City area. Charles Moore, chairman of the National Commission of the Arts, wrote in 1929:

"After two years of study, in light of the finest examples the world has produced, this commission reinstated the authority of the L'Enfant plan and carried it to its logical conclusion in new territory. The action reflected credit not only on the genius of L'Enfant, but also on the commission itself which had the wisdom to recognize the extreme merit of the original plan and the sense—and modesty —to build upon it."*

In 1909, a grateful Washington paid tribute to Pierre Charles L'Enfant in a way that had not been done in his lifetime. His remains

*L'Enfant and Washington, 1929, Johns Hopkins University Press.

were disinterred from their obscure burial place and brought to Jenkins Hill, where he lay in state in the rotunda of the Capitol, an honor reserved for the nation's highest acclaim. He was then reburied in Arlington National Cemetery, high on the hillside overlooking his Federal City. Marking the grave is a granite slab on which is incised a copy of L'Enfant's original conception, a plan which the designer once said "must leave to posterity a grand idea of the patriotic interest which promoted it."

NIGHT TOUR

It is a clear evening in Washington. No clouds are visible, and only a light wind stirs the crisp January air. Shadows dance on the Washington Monument as the flags around its base curl and ripple in the glare of floodlights.

The driver of the tour car is an affable, 50 year old Irishman who has lived in the District of Columbia since 1948. A taxi driver by profession, he works as a commercial guide during his off hours. As is true of most guides in Washington, he is a wealth of miscellaneous information—fact and legend—about the city, its buildings, its memorials, and the people who have made it what it is—everyone, that is, except Jenkins.

The driver goes to several hotels to pick up passengers who have registered in advance for the night tour. It is a small group: three conventioners, a visiting businessman and his wife, a writer, and a seventh man who remains unidentified. The guide maneuvers the car automatically, talking incessantly into a microphone so that all can hear above the noise of the engine and the rattles in the aging, elongated tour machine.

"We are approaching one of the many circles in and around the city—this circle is named for Gen. Winfield Scott, of the Mexican War. The statue of Scott was made of a cannon he captured during the Mexican campaign. The base is carved from a single block of granite, the largest stone ever quarried at that time—1874. Notice how large the general is in comparison to his horse. He was a very big man, weighed over 300 pounds. Some say he always rode small horses..."

"Across the intersection is the old National Geographic Association building, while one block to the right is the new National Geographic Society building. This is considered the finest building built in Washington in the past fifteen years outside of the Kennedy Culture Center. The same architect that did the Kennedy Center and the Georgetown Law School up near the Capitol did this. That is Edward Durell Stone. They have a scientific exhibit on the first floor of the building that is open to the public..."

"On the left is the Russian embassy where the Russian ambassador to the United States lives. The police you see in front are White House policemen. Up until January, 1971, all they had charge of was the security of the White House itself, and the fenced off area around it. The Russian embassy was formerly the home of the Pullman people of railroad fame..."

"We're going to make a left turn at the next intersection, but before we do I want to call your attention to the statue of Andrew Jackson that you see directly in front of us at the end of the street. It is located in the center of Lafayette Park, and is the oldest equestrian statue in the city. It was cast from a cannon captured at Pensacola in Jackson's last campaign there in 1818. Clark Mills, the sculptor, actually trained a horse to rear up like that so he could get the effect he wanted on the statue. It always has been quite controversial because many people say the horse is much too spirited for the relaxed way Jackson is riding it. But Congress must have been impressed, because they voted Mills an extra $20,000 for it in 1853. And the statue is remarkable for its balance—there's a perfect center of gravity in the horse's hind feet..."

"Here is the A.F. of L.-C.I.O. Headquarters. They have a mosaic inside that covers the entire wall. It depicts man's conquest over agriculture and industry. This is the headquarters for the Veterans Administration on the right. To the left on the corner is the United Mine Workers Building, where John L. Lewis spent so many years of his life..."

"We're on Vermont Avenue right now. Look to the left for the Export-Import Bank and the Dolley Madison House, where James and Dolley Madison lived. The National Aeronautics and Space Administration used this as an office building for a time. Here's the new Court of Claims building—the red brick building that we see here in the middle of the block. You'll notice it is L-shaped. They were going to tear down these old houses but President Kennedy and the historical society got after them..."

"Here again is Lafayette Park, right across Pennsylvania Avenue from the White House. The Jackson statue is in the middle of the park, and on each corner is a memorial to someone who helped us during the Revolutionary Period. I don't think there is any other square block in the United States that has more history associated with it than right here. Some of this country's most brilliant politicians, scientists, military men, and literary figures lived here during the early days. The park was set aside by the government in 1791 at the suggestion of George Washington, and it is sometimes called President's Square. Around or near the park are the Tayloe-Cameron House, the Cutts-Madison Mansion, Ashburton House (which is now the St. John's Parish House and once was a British Legation), the Decatur House and Truxton Naval Museum, St. John's Church, and other famous buildings. The statues in the corners of the park are of Generals Lafayette and Rochambleau, who commanded the French Forces in the Revolutionary War, Baron Von Steuben, the Prussian drillmaster of the Revolutionary forces and aide to Washington after Valley Forge, and Thaddeus Kosciuszko, a Polish general who fought with the American Colonists. Lafayette Square was a drill field for Union troops in the Civil War."

Already the mind reels with facts, grasping some, rejecting others ... How many dollars was this statue or that building? ... Decatur—

Decatur, Naval officer, that's it. Shot in a duel at Bladensberg by another officer . . . Are all our heroes generals and other military figures? . . . What's the light bill for Washington? . . . How can we begin to see it all? . . . Who was Jenkins? . . . Yeah, a drill field for troops in one war, and a staging ground for war protesters a century later. Divided country, both times. . .

"Across the intersection to the left is the Treasury Department. They have vaults down in the basement that are operated electrically, and up until the time the vaults were built at Fort Knox, Kentucky, some of the gold bullion was actually stored here. This is the third oldest government building in the city. . ."

"We're going to make a right turn onto Pennsylvania Avenue and coming up on our left is the White House—1600 Pennsylvania Avenue. The White House is the oldest government building in the city. James Hoban, an Irishman, was the architect, and he received first-prize money for his design of the White House in competition with other architects throughout the United States. George Washington was the only President never to live here; John Adams was the first. Then during the War of 1812 with Britain, the British—under Admiral George Cochran—burned both the White House and the Capitol. They later painted the brownstone President's home white in order to hide the fire and smoke spots. It didn't officially get the name White House until Teddy Roosevelt's administration and he had it put on the stationery. Then during President Truman's administration it was completely remodeled at a cost of a little over five and a half million dollars. One of the reasons it cost so much money is that when they took it apart they did it like a jigsaw puzzle, piece by piece. When it was reconstructed it was done the same way—the outside was not touched in any way other than being repaired and painted. . ."

"The flag flies over the White House 24 hours a day by proclamation issued by President Nixon. The White House is open to tourists from 10:00 in the morning until 12:00 noon. It's closed Sundays, Mondays, and holidays. President Jefferson kept the house open two hours a day, too, and anyone who wished to could come see him. Many people were seeking jobs. Presidents don't do that now . . ."

"To the left is the East Entrance of the White House, where the visitors enter. To the right is the west executive wing and this is where the President holds his cabinet meetings and has his private office, swimming pool, bowling alley, and theater. The Rose Garden where Tricia Nixon was married is on the other side of that west executive wing. Mr. Nixon covered the swimming pool and made a press lounge. Out of 132 rooms in the White House, the President actually lives in an apartment-type house on the second floor. . ."

"This is a protest group that we see. There are always three or four different groups protesting—this one is against the Vietnamese War. There is an ordinance that says White House pickets have to keep moving, but they don't enforce it any more since all these demonstrations took place. . ."

"Midway down the block is a house with a green canopy running down from it. This is Blair House, where President Truman lived while the White House was being renovated. And it was here at Blair House that the attempt was made on his life. One guard was killed and two were injured in that attempted assassination. It was here that General Robert E. Lee was offered command of all the Union troops in the field at the beginning of the Civil War—that's right, Robert E. Lee. Of course, he declined and instead took charge of the Southern forces. Lincoln must have been disappointed. Anyway, Blair House is used for guests visiting the White House. That's where Khrushchev stayed when he came to Washington. Next on our right is the building that was built by William Corcoran to house his art collection. Problem was, just when the building was completed, the Civil War broke out and the government borrowed it for offices. When Corcoran finally got it back—several years after the War—he discovered it was too small for his collection, so he built a new gallery. . ."

"I'm going to make a left turn here onto 17th Street. We'll be going directly south on 17th. The building here on the left is the old State, War and Navy Department. It is now used by the executive branch of the government. In other words, this is an office building for the President of the U. S. Mrs. Kennedy led her husband's funeral procession out of the White House on Pennsylvania Avenue, and when they came to this corner on 17th Street they turned right. They went up two and one-half blocks—where 17th Street automatically runs into Connecticut—and then continued up another two and one-half blocks to Rhode Island Avenue and turned right. The second building on the left there is St. Matthew's Cathedral where the funeral service was conducted. After the service, they got into limousines and continued over the same route that we're on right now, down to Constitution Avenue and out Constitution around the Lincoln Memorial, across the Memorial Bridge to Arlington Cemetery. . ."

"Coming up on our right is the Ellipse of the White House, where the nation's Christmas tree is located every year, and looking to the left you'll see the south lawn of the White House and the controversial balcony that was put on by President Truman. This lawn was very popular with the Kennedy family; they used it all the time. Sheep kept the grass cut here during World War I so that groundsmen could be released for more important duties. It's been a golf practice range for at least two presidents: Eisenhower and Harding. John Quincy Adams had quite a garden here, and he collected seeds and nuts from all over to plant where he could care for them. The President's helicopter lands and takes off here on the south lawn. . ."

"Now we'll make a pass by the Federal triangle—nine blocks of government buildings! We'll also go by the statue of General William Tecumseh Sherman, the old Washington Hotel, and the famous Willard Hotel, where the Battle Hymn of the Republic was written. Here's a replica of the Liberty Bell, one of 50 made by the Treasury Department. Now we're turning right onto Pennsylvania Avenue. This is part of the presidential inaugural route—there is the Capitol directly ahead. Here's the old city Post Office. They were going to tear it down, but when they found out how much it would cost to remove it, Congress never appropriated the money. There's talk now that they might tear down the outer part of the building and leave the clock and the tower and build a new building right around it. . ."

"The building under construction ahead of us to the left is to be the new FBI building. It cost $15,000,000 just to purchase the land for this building. With five stories underground, they say that as near as they can figure it, it's going to cost $109,000,000 just to build it . . ."

"Across the intersection to the right is a white marble stone that says in memory of Franklin Delano Roosevelt, the day he was born, and the day he died. It is here more or less on Mr. Roosevelt's own request. He happened to mention to Justice Frankfurter of the Supreme Court that if they ever wanted to erect a memorial to him, all he wanted was a white stone about the size of his desk. He said, 'All I want on it is my name, the day that I was born, and the day that I die. But,' he said, 'I would like it erected in that little, grassy triangle in front of the Archives Building on Pennsylvania Avenue.' The Roosevelt family was here for the dedication of that stone. Coming up on our right is the National Archives Building of the United States, where all the valuable documents of our government are kept. The most valued item here is the original copy of the Constitution of the United States. It's sealed in helium and is displayed on a hydraulic lift. At closing time it goes down into a bomb- and fire-proof vault. The Declaration of Independence and the Bill of Rights are also on display in the building. What we're going to do now is go right to the very end of Pennsylvania Avenue, turn right, and go around the Capitol. By doing that we will have been in all four sections of the city. . ."

"Looking over to the right you see the National Gallery of Art, sometimes called the Mellon Art Gallery. Andrew Mellon, one-time Secretary of the Treasury, paid $15,000,000 to build that building, and afterwards he gave his complete art collection. Directly in front of us is the Capitol. The Capitol is the second oldest government building. The first is the White House, second is the Capitol, third is the Treasury Building. George Washington laid the corner stone with a silver trowel that's on display at the Masonic Memorial over in Alexandria, Virginia. To the extreme right of the Capitol dome is the House of Representatives, and to the extreme left is the Senate chambers. They were added during President Millard Fillmore's administration in 1857. The part underneath the dome is painted to conform with that Massachusetts marble. It's made out of brown sandstone, the same as the White House. If you went up there and actually peeled the paint off that stone, you'd find 117 layers of paint underneath the dome. The dome was added under Lincoln's administration, and it's sometimes referred to as 'the dome that breathes' because it's made out of overlapping steel plates that contract and expand with the weather. At the base of the dome are 36 columns, and each one represents a state in the Union at the time the dome was finished. Up on top there are 13 columns—12 around the outside and one in the middle. They support the statue that's on top of the Capitol dome. It's 'Armed Freedom' by Thomas Crawford—a little over 19 feet and 7½ tons. Now, you'll notice the flagpoles to the left and right of the Capitol

dome. The only time you'll see a flag flying from either one of those poles is when the House or the Senate is in session. Whenever they hold a night session, they turn on a big floodlight at the foot of that statue between the columns. It can be seen over most of the city. . ."

"On our right now is the largest equestrian statue in the United States and the second largest in the world, the memorial to General Ulysses S. Grant, hero of the Civil War. That marble platform is 252 feet long and 69 feet wide, and that's a lot of stone! Henry Shrady spent 19 years of his life on this memorial. Two weeks before it was dedicated, in April, 1922, he died, and Edmond Amateis put the finishing touches on it. Looking to the right you'll notice some group statues of the caissons. They were made from actual photos of the Civil War taken from the Archives. There's a grassy plot of ground here on the right that goes all the way to the Washington Monument, and it's known as the Mall and separates two sections of the city. We're crossing from the northwest section into the southwest section of the city now. . ."

"Looking again at the Capitol: it cost $1,000,000 to build the dome during Lincoln's administration. During Truman's administration they painted it, and it cost almost $1,000,000 to clean and paint it. They sandblasted 108 layers of paint, down to the bare metal. Now they're going to paint it this year at the cost of $85,000, but they're not going to sandblast it. To the left is a memorial to James Garfield, our 20th president, who was assassinated here in Washington by Charles Guiteau, a disappointed office seeker. The three figures at the base of the statue represent the three phases of Garfield's life . . ."

"Ahead of us is the new Sam Rayburn House Office Building, the most expensive office building in the world. It cost us well over $145,000,000—$13,000,000 of that was for two underground parking lots. The next building ahead of us on our right is the Longworth House Office Building. At the top of the hill is the Cannon House Building. All three of these buildings house the 435 Congressmen. The Congressmen from these two buildings are a long way from the Capitol Building and walk by means of a tunnel underneath the street over to the House of Representatives on our left. Across the intersection is the foundation for the new James Madison Memorial Library, an annex to the Library of Congress. As near as they can figure, this building is going to cost $91,000,000 to build. . ."

Let's see—$145,000,000 for the Rayburn Building, $91,000,000 for the Madison Annex, $109,000,000 for the new FBI quarters, plus another $15,000,000 for the land. That adds up to—oh, forget it, that will just spoil the trip!

"Now we are going to stop at the Library of Congress, which is my favorite building here in Washington. It is not a lending library, but anyone can go in and use the facilities. Anything that has been copyrighted will have a copy here. In this building alone there are 200 miles of book shelves. The licensed guides are not allowed to go into the building and lecture to a private group, but let me tell you what to look for. Take the elevator to the balcony inside the dome, where you can look out over the main reading room. Walk back down the marble steps and you'll see on the wall a mosaic to Minerva, the Goddess of Wisdom. There are over 15,000 stones in this mosaic. As you continue down, you'll come to a display area where they have George Washington's family bible and a draft of Lincoln's Gettysburg Address, and Jefferson's draft of the Declaration of Independence. On the main floor of the library, inlaid in brass in the marble floor, are the signs of the Zodiac. When you reach that point, look at the interior of the building. . ."

He didn't do it justice with that description. But then, how could anyone possibly do so?

"Isn't that something else? We're about to cross East Capitol Street now, going from the southeast section to the northeast section. To the right is the United States Supreme Court, the highest court in the land. It's modeled after a Roman temple of Justice, and cost almost $10,000,000 to build in 1935. Just above the eight front columns are the words 'Equal Justice Under Law.' . . ."

"Across the intersection to the right is the New Senate Office Building. Just ahead of us to the left is the Old Senate Office Building. This is where the 100 senators have their offices and committee and hearing rooms. They also have a subway that they ride from these two buildings over to the Senate chambers in the Capitol. You can ride this subway except when you hear a bell ring—that means there is a roll call in the Senate and at that time it's for senators only . . ."

"The intersection just ahead is that of Pennsylvania Avenue and Constitution Avenue. The building under construction to the left is the newest addition to the National Gallery of Art. I think they are starting to overbuild in Washington. One of the things that makes the city unique is that no matter where you look you can see parks and trees, but it's getting to the point where these things are harder to see because all the space is being used for buildings. There is the National Gallery to the left—it is made out of Tennessee pink or rose marble. After it gets wet it actually turns pink; then the sun bleaches it back to white. Across the intersection is the National Archives again. This was dedicated by President Herbert Hoover; John Russell Pope was the architect. On this side of the building are the largest sliding barn doors in the United States. They're 33 feet high, 11½ inches thick, and weigh 6½ tons. . ."

"We're coming to the Arts and Industries Museum of the Smithsonian Institute. It's the second oldest of the Smithsonian group. If you were to walk in this building, you'd see hanging from the ceiling behind the entrance the Wright Brothers' plane, Kitty Hawk, and behind that Lindbergh's Spirit of St. Louis, and a model of an Apollo space ship that landed on the moon. Right behind that is one of the lunar rocks the astronauts brought back, and many other things pertaining to the air and space age. A new Air and Space Museum is being built between 7th and 4th Streets. Across the intersection to the left is the Museum of Natural History of the Smithsonian Institute. In this building they have bones of prehistoric animals, and life-like replicas of men and animals. There is also a display of rare jewels—the Hope diamond can be seen here. . ."

"This is the Bureau of Internal Revenue that we are passing. Income tax. I guess I won't mention that again until after April. It makes people think, 'Oooh, this is it.' . . ."

"On our right now is the newest and most popular of the Smithsonian buildings, the Museum of History and Technology. This building, more than any other in Washington, shows American progress. It has all the gowns worn by First Ladies at inaugural balls, early autos, early locomotives. There are 50 flagpoles around the building, and they fly the state flags in alphabetical order, beginning with Alabama. This building is also made out of Tennessee pink or rose marble, but it must have more pores in it, because it is more of a pinkish color than the National Gallery. . ."

"Here is the Department of Commerce—this is the 14th Street Entrance. They have a fresh water aquarium that is open to the public, and an ever-changing census board that gives you the approximate census of the United States at any given moment. . ."

"Looking ahead and to the left is the memorial to George Washington, the Washington Monument. It started out as a private enterprise. The corner stone was laid in 1848, and when they reached a height of 156 feet they ran out of funds. The work was stopped for 25 years. Finally, during President Grant's administration, Congress appropriated enough money to finish the job, and it was opened to the public in 1885. The monument is 555 feet, 5⅛ inches high, and weighs over 81,000 tons. The capstone alone weighs over 3,300 pounds. There are 898 steps in the monument, and 50 platforms 10 feet apart. The observation windows are at the 500-foot level. There is one elevator, and it takes 30 to 35 people—depending on their size—70 seconds to reach the top. There are 50 flagpoles around the monument, each representing one of the states. They all fly the American flag. The monument is open from 9:00 to 5:00 during the winter months, and 9:00 to midnight in the summer. In the summer there is anywhere from a 30- to 45-minute wait to get up in the elevator. If you'll look along the monument, you'll notice Father Time's mark on the memorial. Although the stone came from the same quarry over in Baltimore County, it didn't match exactly, so Father Time left his mark on the memorial at 156 feet. . ."

"Ahead and to the far left—that building that looks like a red-stone castle—is the first Smithsonian Building here in the United States. The Smithsonian is named after an Englishman, James Smithson, who never set foot on American soil. He had a little trouble with the British government about his birthright and about some scientific papers he wanted published. He went to Italy, and became quite wealthy. Before he died, he inquired if the United States would build an institution of the type he had in mind. The only stipulation was that it carry the name Smithson. So, although he had never been to this country, his body was disinterred in Italy where he died, brought to America, and placed in a sarcophagus just inside the main administration building. . ."

"If you have in mind seeing everything in the Smithsonian, be prepared for a long stay. It has been estimated that if you spend one minute for eight hours a day, seven days a week, looking at each thing that has been catalogued and exhibited, it would take you 10 years to see all the items displayed. . ."

"We're back on the Mall again. This has had many uses over the years, including barracks for troops and houses of ill repute. We're passing now from the northwest section to the southwest section. . ."

"Concealed by the shrubbery and trees here to the right is the Sylvan Theater, an outdoor theater. They hold three outdoor plays here—mainly Shakespearean—during the summer months. Whenever there is a large demonstration here in Washington, they allow the demonstrators to use the theater because it isolates them from the rest of the city. We're travelling on 15th Street, and this is Independence Avenue that we are about to cross. There are only two states that did not have avenues named after them in Washington: they are California and Ohio. There is a beautiful Ohio Drive by the Lincoln Memorial and a California Street in the northwest section of the city. Hawaii and Alaska already had avenues named for them before they became states. Directly in front of us and to the right is the dome of the Jefferson Memorial, erected in honor of the third president. John Russell Pope, the same man who was the architect of the National Archives Building, designed the memorial. Rudolph Evans sculptured Jefferson standing. The statue is a little over 19 feet high. President Franklin D. Roosevelt dedicated that memorial. . ."

"Ahead of us and to the left—the building with all the columns lit up—is the Bureau of Engraving and Printing. This is the only place in the world where the United States paper money is made—legally! All our government bonds and postage stamps are printed here at the Bureau. They have a walking tour during the daytime, but they don't give out samples of their work . . . not even seconds. . ."

"Looking again at the Jefferson Memorial, you'll see a body of water in front of it. This is known as the Tidal Basin. It was built by the Army Engineers, and it takes care of the overflow from the Potomac River. The famous Japanese cherry trees are located around the Tidal Basin. They are a flowering tree only and bear no fruit. They usually bloom the first two weeks of April, and the blossoms last for about 10 days. They are very pinkish when they come out, but then turn snow white. Approximately 600 of the trees were planted around the Tidal Basin. The first was planted by President Taft's wife, and the second by the wife of the Japanese ambassador to the United States. It is our first real sign of spring when the trees blossom. It's really a very beautiful sight. The Jefferson Memorial was built almost entirely on reclaimed land. At one time it was either river land or swamp land. Some of the marble steps were a foot and and a half higher than others three years ago, and they had to remove the marble and put wooden steps in so that people could walk up and down. The landscaped area was gradually settling back down into the swamp. The foundation for the memorial is very sound. When they opened it again in January, 1971—it had been closed all of 1970—they stopped allowing the automobiles and buses to go in front, so we'll have to park back here and you can walk around. . ."

"One time I was waiting here for the people to come back, and these two fellows walked up, and one said, 'Do you mind if we talk to you?' Boy, I thought I'd had it—one was in front and the other was at my side. Then one pulls out a badge and says, 'We're with the FBI. We have that car over there under surveillance, and we want it to look natural.' I really thought they had me. But it's very unusual for anything to happen around the memorials. You hear of crime being so bad in Washington, but it depends on what area you're going into. But around the memorials, it's very unusual. . ."

"As we go along here through West Potomac Park, we'll get a very good view of the Lee mansion across the Potomac River in Arlington. There it is now. You can see the Memorial Bridge where we'll be crossing. That group that I mentioned that was here to disrupt the government was camped all through here. It was cold for three nights—this was back in June—and they tore apart all the wooden benches like those you see here and burned them the first night. They had hundreds of small fires burning out here. The second night it was still cold, so they finished up the benches around the Lincoln, Jefferson, and Washington memorials, then started on the branches of the trees. And further down, as we'll see in a few minutes, is where a construction company is putting in a storm sewer, and because they planned on being there a year and a half or so they put in an expensive picket fence around a couple of acres of land. The demonstrators tore that down and burned it. You come through here with a bus, and with cars parked on both sides it was sometimes just a single lane through here. They'd stand in front of the bus and come over and hold out cans for donations to get their friends out of jail. It was surprising that there were so many kids in that category, or whatever you want to call it. There were thousands of them, and the troops had to be called out—there just weren't enough policemen to cope with them. They slept with just a sheet over them, or in sleeping bags—ah, it was really a mess. They tried to block the bridges to keep the government workers from coming to work and so on. But it didn't work out. . ."

"We're looking at the Lincoln Memorial directly in front of us. The first time the memorial was lit up at night was during the inauguration of President Nixon. Prior to that all that was lighted was the statue of Lincoln in the memorial. There are 36 columns around the memorial, and each one represents a state in the Union during Lincoln's administration. At the top of each column is the name of the state. The Roman numerals mark the date that state entered the Union. Then around the top are 48 memorial festoons with the names of the 48 states at the time it was dedicated. The corner stone was laid in 1915, and the memorial was dedicated in 1922. Chief Justice Taft was head of the Fine Arts Commission then, and he presented the memorial to President Harding, who accepted it on behalf of the American people. Robert Todd Lincoln was present for the dedication. He died in 1926 and is buried just across the river in Arlington. Henry Bacon was the architect for the building; Jules Guerin did the murals Emancipation and Reunion on the inside of the memorial.

Lincoln's Second Inaugural Address and his Gettysburg Address are engraved on the walls. Daniel Chester French was the sculptor of the statute. It is of Lincoln seated, and is just a little over 19 feet high—the chair itself is 12 feet high. It is built on such a scale that if Lincoln were to stand up, he would be 28 feet high. Several blocks of Georgia marble were used for the statue, but they interlock so perfectly that it looks like it was cut from one stone. It took the stone cutters four years to complete the work from French's model. . ."

"It is here to the right in this park where Resurrection City was located during the Poor People's Campaign. This is where they were camped in their plywood shanties, as they wanted them called. There were hundreds of them. . ."

"There is a reflecting pool in front of the memorial. It's 1,000 feet long, 18 inches deep, and is painted black. From this end you can see the Washington Monument when the wind is not blowing, and from the other end the Lincoln Memorial. It's patterned somewhat after the Taj Mahal in India. In winter when it freezes over, people use it for ice skating. . ."

"Directly in front of us now is the new John F. Kennedy Center for the Performing Arts. It was dedicated September 8, 1971. It cost a little over $66,500,000, and that was cutting the budget to the bone. It is three and one-half city blocks long, a block and a half wide, and there is room for 1,400 cars to park in the basement. There is a restaurant up on the roof that seats 800 people. The Center has three theaters right now: the Eisenhower Drama Theater, the Concert Hall, and an Opera House. All three of them can hold performances at the same time. These are the main entrances that we see as we go by. They lead into the Hall of Flags, which in one end has flags of all the nations recognized by the United States, and in the other end has the flags of the 50 states. . ."

"These are the Statues of Peace directly ahead, Arts and Literature. And at the bridge we are about to cross are the Statues of War, Sacrifice and Valor. These were given by the Italian people in appreciation of the Marshall Aid. There is almost $50,000 of gold paint on these statues, and the art of putting it on is considered almost a lost art. The statues came up the river by barge, and were hoisted into position. . ."

"We're about to cross the Potomac River on the Arlington Memorial Bridge—better known as the Lincoln Memorial Bridge. This is the route the funeral processions of both President Kennedy and Robert Kennedy took on the way to Arlington National Cemetery. Looking ahead on the hillside is the Arlington House, which was built in 1802 by George Washington Parke Custis, the adopted son of George Washington. Robert E. Lee married his daughter, Mary Custis, and that is how he acquired the plantation here in Arlington. The house is generally known as the Custis-Lee Mansion. About halfway down the hill, in the cemetery, you will see a light, and if you stare at it, you'll see that it is flickering. That is the Eternal Flame on the grave of President John F. Kennedy. Robert Kennedy is buried roughly 125 feet to the left of that flame. In March, 1966, at 2:00 in the morning, the bodies of President Kennedy and his two children were disinterred and moved about 40 feet down the hillside from where they were originally buried. On that same morning, at about 7:00, Mrs. Kennedy, members of the Kennedy family, Cardinal Cushing, President Lyndon Johnson, just to mention a few, were here for the reinternment in this permanent memorial. This memorial cost a little over a million and a half dollars. The Eternal Flame that Robert Kennedy and Mrs. Kennedy lit at his original burial was also moved. . ."

"Arlington National Cemetery was started during the Civil War when this area was occupied by Union forces. It was also used as a hospital area by Union forces. During the Civil War notice was posted that anyone owning property in Virginia had to pay their taxes in person, in the hope that General Lee would come in and get captured. Well, naturally he didn't do it. But his wife, Mary Custis Lee, did send in the tax money with one of the servants, but it was refused by the federal government. So the property was sold for delinquent taxes during the Civil War and the government bought it for $26,500 at the tax sale. After the war, Robert E. Lee made no attempt whatsoever to buy back the property or to get it back through the courts. He went to Lexington, Virginia, and became president of Washington University there. He died there, and is buried in the university chapel alongside his father, Light Horse Harry Lee. The university is now known as Washington and Lee University. After his death, Lee's son brought suit against the government for the property, saying that the tax sale during the Civil War was illegal. The case went to the Supreme Court, and they ruled in favor of Lee's son. He received $150,000 in compensation. He then assigned a clear deed to the property here in Arlington. . ."

The tour continues, and the guide rambles on—more facts, more costs, quotations, anecdotes, tales. Here is the Tomb of the Unknowns; now the Pentagon, with its 17½ miles of corridors and square dancing every Tuesday and Thursday night; the Netherlands Carillon; the Iwo Jima Marine Memorial, which at 100 tons is the largest bronze statuary ever cast. By now the visitor is totally overwhelmed, and yet so little of this fabulous city has been visited.

THE WHITE HOUSE

"Good morning, ladies and gentlemen. On behalf of the President and Mrs. Nixon, I'd like to welcome you to the White House. When you came in I'm sure you saw the sign outside asking no smoking and no pictures. While we're in the house there are a few rules we all have to follow. Please do not sit on or use any of the furnishings—they date back to about 1800 and are irreplaceable."

The guide is a young, Jack-Armstrongish type, who speaks with a pleasant southern drawl. He identifies himself as an officer of the Executive Protective Service. This is the special tour, which takes place about an hour and a half before the house is opened for regular visitors. It takes some sort of contact to get a reservation for this tour, and probably all 200 or so of those here were wondering the same thing while waiting outside the gate: "If this is a special tour, what is it like during regular visitation?"

"When you came into the house this morning you entered through the East Wing, which was added in 1942 to take care of the growing staff of Franklin D. Roosevelt after the declaration of World War II. You came up along the promenade and outside the glass doors there is the Jacqueline Kennedy Garden, dedicated to Mrs. Kennedy by President Johnson in 1965."

You noticed, if you were looking, a piece of paper torn out of a notebook, taped to the glass doors which said: 'Don't use this door. Lock broken.' Someone should tell the man of the house to fix it.

"The construction on the house started in 1792, and it wasn't completed when President John Adams moved in in 1800. George Washington was the only president not to live in the house. When the house was burned by the British in 1814, it had to be reconstructed. President Monroe moved in in 1817, and because of the fire he had to make the largest purchases of any president in office. Several of the pieces he purchased are still being used in the house and you will see those today.

"The house underwent a major renovation in 1902 and at that time the West Wing was added. However, the Oval Office wasn't added until 1909. Then again from 1948 to 1952 the residence received another renovation. The entire interior was taken out and the walls were reinforced with steel and concrete. Then the house was put back in the same fashion it was before.

"Now, there's actually six floors to the house, with two basements beneath it. We will be seeing the stage floor, the ground floor that we are on now, and the first floor that is above. These are the floors that are used during all the functions and parties that take place here in the White House. The second floor is the personal residence of the First Family, and the third floor is somewhat similar to a hotel, with several bedrooms that are used for guests who stay overnight in the White House."

And this is one hotel that honestly can say, "President Lincoln slept here." And Grant, Garfield, Polk, Fillmore, and 31 others. Do they tip the maids?

"Because of the size of the group we won't be able to go into the two rooms next to us. On your right is the White House Library, which contains about 2,800 volumes of Americana, including several volumes written by former presidents. Incidentally, the paneling on the walls was made from beams that were placed in the house in 1817 and removed during the renovation in the 1950's. The furniture in this room is primarily Duncan Phyfe, and that cane-back couch on the other side of the room is one of the finest examples of the period. Now, the chandelier is English cut glass and red tole, and it once belonged to the family of James Fenimore Cooper.

"Above the mantel is the familiar portrait of George Washington by Gilbert Stuart. That is the one you frequently see reproduced in our history books. Now, across the hall is the Vermeil Room. Vermeil

is a French invention of gold fired on silver. This collection was donated to the house in 1956 by Margaret Thompson Biddle, and the pieces in here are used occasionally for state dinners. The painting above the mantel is 'Morning on the Seine' by Claude Monet, which was donated to the house by the Kennedy Family in memory of President John F. Kennedy. For those of you who couldn't see, take a glance as we go by. We'll go on now to the China Room."

What is the aura of the White House? In part, it has to be the knowledge that this is the home and the office of the President of the United States, and it represents the awesome responsibility, formality, dignity, and all other ramifications that go with being a chief of state. Yet this is a living house: real people live and have lived here, have laughed, danced, played, fought, loved, cried, and shouted.

We have passed through the Diplomatic Reception Room, with its remarkable hand-painted wall paper, Zuber's "Scenic America." The artist did the work in 1834, and the paper was found on the walls of a mansion in Maryland about to be torn down. An alert college student with a sense of history rescued the paper. The guide says the student purchased it for a few dollars, took it from the walls, and brought it to the White House in baskets, where he sold it for several dollars. Good for him!

Here now is the East Room, the largest room in the White House, where Abigail Adams hung her wash, Abraham Lincoln housed troops, Nellie Grant and Lynda Bird Johnson were married, and Richard Nixon signed the most recent amendment to the Constitution, giving the franchise to America's 18-year-old citizens. Now the guide is telling how Dolley Madison saved the famous painting of George Washington when the British sacked the White House. He mentions another painting, but neglects to tell that the other portrait she saved was a portrait of Dolley Madison! (He also doesn't mention the fact that General Ross, who with Admiral Cochran led the British forces into Washington, later was quoted as saying he would not have fired the White House had Mrs. Madison remained there. Ross reportedly said: "I make no war on letters and ladies," and also, "I have heard so much praise of Mrs. Madison that I would rather protect than burn a house that sheltered so excellent a lady..." But who is to fault her for fleeing, with the enemy at her door?)

Now the Green Room, restored as a parlor of the 1800's, distinct for its American furniture and the dark green silk wall coverings. Everywhere there are art treasures—clocks, paintings, sculpture. Now to the Blue Room, often considered the most beautiful in the house, and a frequent selection for receptions. This room was the choice of Grover Cleveland for his wedding to Frances Folsom, the only marriage of a president to take place in the White House. Now the Red Room, long considered a favorite by First Ladies. As with the other rooms, the incredible artwork:

"The painting that you see above the doorway is John James Audubon, after whom the Audubon Society was named. On the opposite side of the room, you see above the doorway President

Pierce done by George Healy, and in the center of the room Col. William Dryden—that was painted by Samuel F. B. Morse. Beneath that is the 'Last of the Mohicans' by Asher B. Durand. Above the doorway is James Polk, also by Healy. Now, I mentioned that there was one other portrait besides Stuart's 'Washington' that was here prior to the fire. And it is that portrait of Dolley Madison, also painted by Gilbert Stuart. She saved Washington's portrait, but she also managed to save her own!"

Good fellow, he wasn't holding back on us after all—just a matter of timing. Now we pass on to the State Dining Room, which can be described merely as magnificent. Here one has to agree with the words of John Adams, which Theodore Roosevelt had inscribed on the mantel:

"I pray Heaven to Bestow the Best of Blessings on this House and on All that shall hereafter Inhabit it. May none but Honest and Wise Men ever rule under this Roof."

This must be the room in which John Kennedy entertained 29 Nobel Prize winners and made his famous toast to "the most extraordinary collection of talent, of human knowledge, that has ever been gathered together at the White House, with the possible exception of when Thomas Jefferson dined alone."

"Now we will move out into the North Entrance. Whenever there is a visiting head of state staying overnight in Washington, he will stay across the street in the Blair House. He will come to the White House by limousine, come in through the North Entrance, and will meet with the President up in the Yellow Oval Room, which is directly above the Blue Room. They will exchange gifts there, then they will come down the Grand Stairway and have pictures taken. The Marine Band, which is the President's Band, will be standing in front of that large mirror, and the band will play 'Ruffles and Flourishes' and 'Hail to the Chief' as the party moves on into the State Dining Room or the East Room, depending on where the function is to be held. During Tricia Nixon's wedding in June, a large cake was set here in front of the mirror. She threw her bouquet from the stairway and the wedding party left out the North Entrance and down the driveway which you will be going down this morning. Portraits of the past six presidents have been placed here in the North Entrance. Directly behind me you see President Johnson, done by Elizabeth Shoumatoff, and in the entranceway you see President Kennedy, by Aaron Shickler. Across the hall there is President Truman, and at the opposite end, President Eisenhower. On the first landing of the stairway is President Hoover and then President Franklin D. Roosevelt. Now, this is going to conclude my talk with you, and if you have any questions as you are going out, there will be a man standing at the doorway to answer them for you. Thank you all very much for coming today."

Some pad!

POLITICAL WASHINGTON

To most Americans, political Washington brings to mind the President and the Congress, as well it should, because the executive and legislative branches of the government wield an authority that is unique to the city and the District.

The city and the District—are they different? Not really, at least not in terms of political subdivision. Washington and the District are one and the same and the government of the city is, in fact, the government of the District of Columbia. And the District of Columbia is a political subdivision unlike any other in the United States. At the same time, it is a combination of all other political subdivisions.

Confusing? Yes. Martin K. Schaller, executive secretary for the District of Columbia and to Walter Washington, the mayor of Washington, explains the relationship this way:

"The District of Columbia is a state, a county, and a city all in one, and the mayor exercises many of the functions of a governor, county executive, and mayor. We have almost all the governmental functions that you would find in a state, a county, and a city. For instance, there is no other city in the United States that has a department of motor vehicles. That is always a state function. No city government has a department of insurance. That also is a state function. Boards of education operate on city, county, and state levels, so our superintendent of education would be a commissioner of education in a state government. We are in competition with all the states for federal grants, and this is one of the 'governor' functions that the mayor exercises. We have a district income tax that is analogous with a state tax, and a D. C. real estate tax, a personal property tax, and other minor taxes—motor vehicle, tobacco, alcohol, business inventory, business franchise, and so on."

Some of the confusion about the political subdivision of the region has existed since the establishment of the District of Columbia. The original District was made up of approximately 68 square miles of the State of Maryland and 32 square miles of the State of Virginia. Included within those boundaries were five separate political entities: the existing cities of Georgetown (Maryland) and Alexandria (Virginia); the new Federal City being planned by Pierre L'Enfant; the county of Washington, which was all the area outside of Georgetown and the City of Washington in the State of Maryland; and the County of Alexandria, that area outside of the City of Alexandria in Virginia. In 1846, Congress returned the 32 square miles of land in Virginia to that state, reducing the size of the District of Columbia to the 68 square miles in the boundaries of Maryland, and comprising three political subdivisions: Georgetown, the City of Washington, and the County of Washington. In 1895, Congress merged Georgetown with the City of Washington, ending the former's status as a separate city.

Since its inception, the District of Columbia has had various types of government. From 1800 to 1871, commissioners or mayor-city council types of government existed. But in 1871, Congress made a historical change when it declared the District a legal *territory*, just like other territories before they became states, with a governor, a two-chamber territorial legislature, and a delegate to the U. S. House of Representatives. Even then the District was not self-governing: the governor was appointed, as was one house in the legislature. The other house was elected by citizens of the District. But Congress ended the territorial period in 1875 when it felt the governor was exercising too much authority, and put in its place an appointed board of commissioners.

In 1967, Congress established the present mayor-city council form of government in the District of Columbia. Residents of the District still do not vote for their officials, for the mayor and the nine-man council are appointed by the President and must be confirmed by the Senate. However, some franchise opportunity has come to the District of Columbia in the last decade: in 1964 the citizens of the District were able to vote for the President of the United States for the first time. Citizens also elect their school board and, since 1970, elect a delegate to the House of Representatives who has a vote in committee although not on the floor of the House.

One of the biggest problems facing the residents of the District of Columbia is that of "home rule," the ability of the citizens to decide for themselves the type of local government officials they shall have. Home rule means different things to different people, and it might be difficult to get agreement in the District as to what is needed. But to all it means that there should be some means of popular election of the officials of the District of Columbia.

At the present time, the Congress exercises 100 percent review power of the budget of the mayor of Washington, even though approximately 75 to 80 percent of the budget funds are raised by taxation of the citizens and have nothing to do with federal revenues. The federal revenues—20 to 25 percent of the total budget package for the District—are monies received in part in lieu of taxation on the 45 percent of the land in the District which is owned by the federal government and is not revenue-producing—in other words, the monumental area of the District. In addition, the federal monies provided to the District of Columbia also represent assistance for services performed: police and fire services, sanitation services, sewer and water, highways, and other similar services.

Washington would not be self-sufficient without the federal revenues. The city has no large industries. The business of government is the main business in the city, and provides the primary source of revenue. The second biggest business is tourism—about 18,000,000 tourists visit Washington each year, an estimated 1,000,000 more than visit New York City. One and one-half million of those visitors to Washington are from foreign lands.

Some 275,000 federal employees work in the area, and, with another 40,000 city or District employees, make a total of about 315,000 government workers in the District of Columbia. The primary sources of revenue for the District is the income tax, sales tax and property tax.

Congress exercises its influence on the city through the budget revenue process. Four committees of Congress are concerned with the District of Columbia. Each chamber has a subcommittee on Appropriations in the District of Columbia and a Committee on the District of Columbia. These latter committees are concerned with revenue and other legislation and have the tax-making authority. The only tax-making authority residing with the council is the power to raise and lower the District of Columbia real estate tax. All other revenue raising authority rests with the Congress. Ultimately, Congress will make the decision on home rule for the District, if such a decision is forthcoming.

Schaller and other officials in the District predict that home rule is coming. Early in 1972, the mayor's assistant commented:

"Home rule has been progressing since 1964. It hasn't gone fast enough for the citizens in the city or those in the government who think we should have home rule, but the process is a slow and complex one. I think we'll have some sort of home rule within two to five years.

EMERGENCE

"Washington is emerging from the cultural Boondocks."

This was the opinion of Richard L. Coe, influential critic for *The Washington Post* in mid-1971. The cause of Mr. Coe's appraisal was the operation of eight professional theaters in the city and its near environs. Coe noted:

"While Los Angeles and Chicago may possibly have as much stage action, Washington clearly ranks second to New York as the land's most active theater area."

Coe's remarks were written prior to the opening of the Kennedy Center for the Performing Arts, which added a ninth professional theater to the Washington scene. This count did not include three summer theaters: Olney, Shady Grove, and the unique Wolf Trap Farm Park, located just outside the city. Nor did he include several dinner theaters now operating in the Washington suburban area.

Queen of Washington's theaters is the National Theater, which has been in existence since 1835. The National is where the Broadway stars and productions traditionally have played in Washington. Because of its location and the quality of its billing, the National has not been affected by the opening of the Kennedy Center.

While the National Theater may be the queen, the new Kennedy Center has been called the "cultural crown" for the nation's capital. Here, under one roof, are an elegant concert hall, seating nearly 2,800 persons, an opera house with one of the largest stages in the world, the Eisenhower theater, and a small movie theater that is convertible for live theater productions. In all, the Kennedy Center can seat more than 6,500 persons at one time, nearly the same amount of seating as all of the other theaters combined.

The Kennedy Center is one of the living memorials in the nation's capital dedicated to the performing arts. The other is Ford's theater.

By day, Ford's is the theater where Lincoln was shot, and by night, the theater that Lincoln loved.

Ford's was closed in 1865 when President Lincoln was shot there. An attempt by the owner to open the building a few months after the assassination met with such protest that the idea was abandoned, and the building was purchased by the government for use as offices and storage. In 1932, the Lincoln Museum was opened in the basement of the building, featuring the astounding Oldroyd Collection of Lincolniana. Later many items associated with the assassination which had been held in storage were added to the museum. In 1964, Congress appropriated funds to restore the theater and reopen it for stage productions, a decision that should have pleased the martyred president. Today, in its dual role, Ford's Theater is one of Washington's most intriguing buildings.

Though the theater has been renovated and restored to look and feel like it was more than a century ago, Ford's bright young manager, Edward Yoe, introduced Washington to "Ticketron," a computerized ticket sales method with outlets at neighboring shopping centers, as up-to-date as Ford's contemporary drama.

Not to be overlooked in the dazzle of the Kennedy Center, the intrigue of Ford's, and the charm of National is Washington's noted theater in the round, the Arena Stage, which operates in a new building in the city's renewed southwest district. This theater is now recognized as one of the country's most successful repertory theaters.

Exemplary of Washington area dinner theaters is Hayloft Theater, located in Virginia near the Manassas-Bull Run Battle Field. Hayloft is somewhat of a cultural phenomenon, providing professional theater in the suburbs. It is friendly, intimate, with superb cuisine prepared under the direction of Nassib Georges Richa, former chef for the Belgian embassy and the U. S. State Department. Experiencing Hayloft is a rare epicurean and theatrical treat. It is one of six dinner theaters in the Washington area, all of which have been started in the last four years.

Wolf Trap Park for the Performing Arts is located in Virginia, 17 miles from Washington. This is the first national park for the arts, and will have resident cottages for resident composers and writers in addition to the outdoor stage.

Can Washington support nine professional theaters, six dinner theaters (some of which also have professional companies), an opera house, concert hall, and a multitude of small recital halls and theaters? Mrs. Jouett Shouse, patroness of the arts in Washington, believes there is widespread demand for the performing arts in the capital, and that the more available, the more the audience develops. Mrs. Shouse says:

"We are all doing better. It is possible to fill the Kennedy Center's three theaters as well as Wolf Trap, all on the same night, if what is being presented is good.

"We have a very selective audience here in Washington, and they know what is good and what isn't. They do not patronize the things that are not worth going to see. This is the challenge to all people who play here."

Mrs. Shouse feels that Washington is becoming the cultural capital of the country, as well as the political capital. She comments:

"All we need is a very fine music school which we don't have now. But that will come. Within 20 years, Washington will be the cultural capital."

With more than 200 libraries, untold museums and art galleries, incredible historical sites, concert halls, and now the most active theater outside of New York, one wonders if Washington has not already earned the title of cultural capital of the nation. Regardless, the multitude of attractions underscores the obvious conclusion that there is something for everyone in Washington.

ANOTHER WASHINGTON

Washington is a monumental city, where more than 600 statues, markers, and memorials pay homage to native- and foreign-born heroes who have placed an immortal stone in the mosaic of the nation's history.

But Washington is another city, too. It is the home of some 750,000 persons, most of whom are black, and the place of business for thousands more who arrive daily from nearby suburban communities.

For the most part, citizens in Washington go about the business of living without any great show of concern for the many memorials to America's history and heritage.

Some citizens who live in Washington have very little regard for the awesomeness of being in the nation's capital. There are adults and school children in Washington who have never stepped inside a memorial, never visited any part of the Smithsonian, and who think the National Theater is a movie house. Such generalizations obviously do not include *all* citizens of Washington, for as a group they may well be the most informed, most aware populace in the nation.

Do the memorials go unnoticed by those who live and work in the District of Columbia? Are they a mockery to the city's black citizens? One black, a staff member of the district government, answers:

"Not necessarily a mockery, because the basic theme and thesis of America is good and can be embraced. The only thing is, as a black you have problems cashing your check at the bank of justice. That's how a lot of black people see Washington, D.C.—and not necessarily just Washington, but the United States. They see Washington as an extension and a manifestation of America. It is the nature of blacks in the United States, in terms of where black citizens stand in the total structure or system, to have a certain kind of reservation about even participating in the enjoyment and upkeep and revelling of those kinds of monuments.

Another city employee, who is white, comments:

"When I first came here I could look out the window and see the Capitol dome, which was about six blocks from where I was working. It really got me. You know, it was something you saw on TV or in the

history books. The feeling lasted about a year. Now I drive by the Capitol and don't even think about it.

Still another Washingtonian has this to say about her adopted city:

"I like Washington as a city. There are many jobs here if you are qualified for them; shopping is convenient. Banks and supermarkets will cash your checks. There are many stores where you can choose different varieties of clothing and shoes, find something that no one else has.

Peggy Haynes is a small, soft-voiced, attractive black, who has trained and worked as a private secretary, but who is assistant manager of the donut store. She is reserved, and a bit cautious about answering the questions of a stranger:

"I take advantage of the city. I go to the theater, shows, and ball games. I came from a small town, and it is just great to be able to go see the movies when they first come out, or hear music when it is released. I used to read about things months before they would get to my town."

Like most people in Washington, Miss Haynes toured the monuments and the White House when she first moved to the city. She found the experience educational. She still likes to drive around or get out and walk around some of the historic sites.

"I like the Lincoln Memorial best of the monuments. I especially like to go there in the spring, when you can sit on the grass or on the steps and just look around, get the mood of the people. I just think it is fantastic the way it is set up—the statue, the pictures, and his writings.

"You don't see a lot of Washington people around the memorials usually, unless they have visitors from out of town. When people come to visit they always want to see Washington and all the things they have read about all their lives.

"I guess the only real problem here is that the cost of living is extremely high. But if you work and make good money, you can afford to have nice things. I'm never going to buy nice things, though, 'cause my apartment's always getting robbed. Three times so far. But, I'll stay here as long as I can—you know, as long as no one tries to kill me."

The high crime rate is just one of the problems plaguing the city. Whether or not deserved, Washington has a reputation as being unsafe. Hotels and motels display signs warning visitors not to venture out alone at night, and admonishing guests to lock their doors at all times. But major crimes actually declined in the city last year, due both to the high profile of the city's police force and an extensive lighting program. Since October, 1970 the city has been installing high-intensity sodium vapor lights downtown and in the areas of repeated felonies, and in some locations lighting alone is credited with cutting crime rate forty to sixty percent. One city official estimates that about sixty percent of Washington's crimes are drug related, and that there are some 20,000 hard-drug addicts in the District of Columbia alone. While discouraging at first glance, these figures give a perspective as to the solution of the problem.

Most of Washington's urban difficulties are the same as can be found in any other major metropolitan area: unemployment, overpopulation, pollution, urban sprawl, heavy traffic, poverty. But an awareness of what happens on Capitol Hill tends to expose the great paradox of Washington: Congress spends billions of dollars on highways, skyways, war, defense, space shots, and foreign aid while nearby are hundreds of hungry citizens.

That paradox is evident in the physical Washington, too. Minutes from the White House, with its glistening paint and manicured lawns, are once-proud brownstone houses with sparse and parched lawns, broken windows, and blistered paint. Many places that once were single family dwellings have been divided into flats now housing one or more families on each floor.

But even though there is a preponderance of bureaucracy through which to work, Washington officials believe the city's problems are solvable. Credit is given to the leadership of Walter Washington, the city's black mayor, who has brought positive gains to the city under the most trying circumstances. The mayor must respond to the White House and to the Congress; he must respond to the black middle class and the black militant element; he must respond to the white affluent and the white businessman. At all times he has pressure being exerted on him in a variety of ways, but he has been able to keep the people in mind in the operation of the city. The mayor has made a genuine attempt to have a city government responsive to all people, not just one particular element or segment.

Washington, indeed, is a city where historical romanticism chafes against the ragged edges of urban realities. The success or failure of this city to solve its problems will be either a classic model or a horrible example for the entire nation.

D. C. POTPOURRI

Washington is—a traffic cop who orchestrates the automobile congestion with the grace of a symphony conductor; triangles and mini-parks, bits of green that relieve the pressure of urbanization; trees, trees, trees; bus drivers who think traffic will dissolve with the blast of a horn; weathervanes of every size and description; freeways that encircle the Kennedy Center like a giant serpent; flags, pigeons, squirrels, airplanes; Mr. Z's topless go-go place, five blocks from the Capitol; statues, markers, plaques, monuments, memorials, and inscriptions; joggers on the Mall; columns; high, narrow, oval-topped windows; cupolas; plastic throw-away plates and table service in the Capital restaurant; noise of the METRO construction; radio ads that announce "Pre-freeze prices for cars"; the long, long vigil in front of the White House against the war in Vietnam; the only city in the country where Congress legislates freeways; a mini-court in front of the Anthony House; high, thin, two- and three-story buildings, standing all alone in a block; thunder reverberating forever off the solid walls along federal row; haunting, modernistic, aggregate concrete guitar players in the foyer of the Jefferson building; big trundle cars full of publications pushed down long, freshly-painted corridors in the Senate catacombs; friendly, courteous, helpful Capitol police.

Taste is very much in evidence in the dress of Washingtonians, black and white. They are conservatively and smartly dressed—fashionable.

There is an attractive red-head in a long coat, with oversize sleeves, worn almost like a cape. Now a young black girl in high, tight boots. Here is a lady in a leopard-skin coat, small hat, scarf wound tightly around her neck; there is a slender girl in a knee-length, orange suede coat with brocade trim. These are the styles of the smart, perhaps the wealthy. Minis, midis, maxis, boots, long hair, pants suits—very striking.

In contrast are the long, black overcoats, saggy jeans, drab, old, tattered, beaten clothing. Probably the clothes of the wealthy, too.

The United States Senate is debating Senate 2515, a controversial bit of legislation titled Employment Opportunities Enforcement Act of 1971. This act would establish a commission to investigate alleged infractions of the equal employment act.

Only a few senators are on the floor, and hardly any spectators in the gallery. Senator Harrison Williams, of New Jersey, is concluding his remarks in support of the bill.

"Mr. President, will the Senator yield for some questions?"

Mr. Williams: "I am happy to yield to the Senator from North Carolina."

Senator Sam Ervin: "By this bill, the executive branch of the federal government is given the power to go to the judicial branch of the federal government and ask it to tell state officials who control hiring practices of the state what to do. Is that so?"

Mr. Williams: "It says there shall be no discrimination because of one's color. I will tell the Senator that. It is as clear as it can be."

Mr. Ervin: "Does not the word 'discrimination' mean a preference—if one exercises a preference, is he not practicing a discrimination?"

Mr. Williams: "A prejudice or a preference, put it as you will. I would say a prejudice rather than a preference."

Mr. Ervin: "Those of us who are married proposed to one girl because we preferred her over another. Is that not a discrimination?"

Mr. Williams: "That will be the day when the Senate involves itself in that!"

Two high-school age girls from Texas are standing on the corner near the Capitol. They talk freely about their impressions of Washington. One says:

"It is not what I expected. I really expected to be overwhelmed by the city—you know, all these huge buildings. They weren't as big as I thought. The cops and the black population impressed me more. I'm not used to that. I think that's interesting.

"We're from San Antonio. Houston has quite a few black people, but we don't in San Antonio. For the first time in my life I know a little like what it is like to be in the minority.

"Favorite place? The Jefferson Memorial. That's the greatest. Isn't that memorial amazing? It's fantastic. At night, you sit there, and you read all his stuff on the walls. God!"

One youngster asks, "Who runs this city?" When told that the President appoints the Mayor and the city council, and that Congress must pass on the budget for the city, the response is a meaningful, teen-age "WOW." Not the way you read "WOW," but "WOWOA" —a slow drawl with a depth of meaning that would take ten sentences to express.

"It's a nice city. I haven't been anyplace much larger than this, but you don't get the feeling that this city is giant, congested, dirty, and ugly. It has a neat skyline. Most of it must be fairly new."

THE PENTAGON

Thumbtacked to a bulletin board in the Pentagon:

NOTICE

Placing posters, flyers, notices

or other advertising media on

this board is prohibited.

FEELINGS

Washington is a city that can play havoc with one's feelings. It can happen when you watch the sun set behind the Washington monument, with the spires of the Smithsonian silhouetted against a darkening sky; it can happen before the brooding figure of Abraham Lincoln in the memorial to the man; it can happen as you read Thomas Jefferson's draft of the Declaration of Independence in the handwriting of this astounding being; it can happen when you see fine brownstone houses decaying in dilapidation and ruin only moments from the splendor of the Capitol; it can happen as you stand before the original of the Constitution, faded now in the light of nature, but not in the glory of man; it can happen on the steps of the Capitol, the forge of this democracy.

This emotional city—conceived in compromise, delivered in national insecurity, sacked in war, and reconstituted in victory—is above all a tribute to George Washington, Pierre L'Enfant, Benjamin Banneker, Thomas Jefferson, James Madison, Alexander Shepherd, William Thornton, James Hoban, Benjamin Latrobe, and countless others who have extended genius beyond the normal measure. It is the kind of city to which John Kennedy referred when he said:

"I am certain that after the dust of centuries has passed over our cities, we, too, will be remembered not for our victories or defeats in battle or in politics, but for our contribution to the human spirit."

This is Jenkins Hill today.

Father John Carroll, founder of Georgetown
University, lends stature to entrance of Healy
Building. Georgetown, the oldest Catholic university
in the nation, opened its doors in 1789, the same
year George Washington was inaugurated president
and the first Congress was called into session.

New Executive Office Building from the Jackson Place entrance. An excellent example of contemporary architecture living among the old. Right: The Washington National Monument by Robert Mills renders a spectacular background to people resting and playing in the trees. More than two million people visit this marble obelisk annually.

"Let us therefore animate and encourage each other, and
show the whole world that a freeman, contending for liberty
on his own grounds, is superior to any slavish mercenary on earth."

GEORGE WASHINGTON

Memorial to John Ericson, builder of the Monitor,
and inventor of the screw propeller. It is located
south of the Lincoln Memorial at Ohio Drive. Right:
Closeup depicts the excellent craftsmanship
executed by the Sculptor J. E. Fraser.

A white swan greets the early morning beside the reflecting pool between the Washington and Lincoln Monuments. Right: Strollers walk across the marble courtyard in front of the Supreme Court Building.

"I believe that unarmed truth and unconditional love
will have the final word in reality."

MARTIN LUTHER KING, JR.

The White House, of unmatched beauty in its period,
is a building of simplicity and dignity. Attracted by
its historical significance, more than one million
people visit it each year. Right: Across Pennsylvania
Avenue from the Executive Mansion state flags hang
in honor of a visiting foreign head of state.

A central part of Pierre L'Enfant's original plan was
the Mall. It is an open vista from the Washington
Monument to the Capitol, lined with historical and
cultural institutions that inspire all. Right: The
Jackson statue, by Clark Mills, in LaFayette Square
erected in 1855. Cannon, captured by Jackson in
the War of 1812, supplied the bronze.

"It is the living not the dead, that are to be accommodated."

TOM PAINE

43

Shrine of the Immaculate Conception erected on
the campus of Catholic University in northeast
Washington is one of many impressive religious
buildings that help make Washington a center for
all faiths. Right: Noteworthy design at the entrance
to the Iranian Embassy on Massachusetts Avenue.

Monument to four chaplains by Constantino Nivola and, on the right, Fountain of Faith by Carl Milles, both located in the National Memorial Park, Falls Church, Virginia. In contrast to the equestrian generals, both pieces are notable contemporary sculptures in the Washington area.

Flanking the Capitol to the right are the nonidentical twins, the old Senate and House Office Buildings, commissioned to be a properly subdued background for the Capitol. Right: Flags fly in the wind at the base of the Washington Monument.

48

"There is the national flag. He must be cold, indeed, who can look upon its folds rippling in the breeze without pride of country."

CHARLES SUMNER

Impressive bronze sculpture on the Buffalo Bridge
renders unusual contrast to the strong, geometric
shapes of the Turkish Embassy. Right: Lowering the
colors at the Custiss-Lee Mansion in Arlington
National Cemetery overlooking the Potomac River.
The great city in the distance.

"I can anticipate no greater calamity for the country than a dissolution of the union—still, a union that can only be maintained by swords and bayonets has no charm for me."

GENERAL ROBERT E. LEE

Ornate lamp embellishes the walk and driveways on the east Capitol grounds. It was erected approximately one hundred years ago. Right: Unusual stone carving of Aysh-Ke-Bah-Ke-Ko-Zhay (Flat Mouth), a Chippewa chief, situated on the third floor in the senate wing of the Capitol Building.

A pond lily plant growing in the National Arboretum in northeast Washington. Located in an intermediate climatic zone, a wide range of trees and shrubs thrive in this area. Right: Casual observers visit the Jefferson Memorial on south shore of Tidal Basin.

"No man is good enough, no group of men, to be trusted with unrestrained powers."

THOMAS JEFFERSON

55

The beautiful Washington Cathedral towers above
the very summit of Mt. St. Albans in northwest
Washington. Constructed according to medieval
structural principles, it is one of the great churches
of the world. Right: Enjoying a ride amidst autumn's
brilliant colors in Rock Creek Park near Georgetown.

"The president is there in the white house for you, it is not you
who are there for him, the secretaries act in their bureaus
for you not you here for them, the congress convenes
every twelfth month for you, laws, courts, the forming of
states, the charters of cities, that going and coming of
commerce and mails, are all for you . . ."

WALT WHITMAN

Painting of George Washington by Gilbert Stuart
magnifies wall of the east room in the White House.
It is one of three objects still in evidence since the
house was first occupied in 1800. Right: Lindens
form a hedge against the glassed colonnade north of
the rose garden. The President's office overlooks this
most delightful garden from the west wing.

"May none but honest and wise men ever rule under this roof."

JOHN ADAMS

61

Control tower of Dulles International Airport in nearby Virginia. Eero Saarinen designed this revolutionary airport, truly an abrupt change in air terminal facilities. Right: "Mrs. Joan W. Simpson" by Auguste Rodin, a work in marble located in the National Gallery of Art, a gift from Mrs. Simpson.

Small gardens embellish the colonial charm of
these older homes in the East Capital District.
Right: The Islamic Center, first mosque of authentic
Arabic architecture to be erected in the Western
Hemisphere. The gracefully soaring minaret is
160 feet high. It stands at a slight angle to
Massachusetts Avenue because it is oriented like
every true mosque, to face toward Mecca.

A boat powers its way under the Arlington Memorial
Bridge on the Potomac River with Theodore
Roosevelt Island and Arlington in the background.
Right: A young Washingtonian comes up from a
cooling plunge, reflecting little concern for the heat
or humidity on a midsummer day.

One of two great golden coated statues on the east
end of the Arlington Memorial Bridge. They were a
gift from the people of Italy to the people of
the United States. Right: Historic Georgetown, a
district of elegant townhouses and comfortable
living, was a thriving community when the capital
city was but rolling hills of woodland.

Artist demonstrates her technique with a live model
surrounded by an interested group in a park near
the Ellipse. Right: Canoers seek plant life on Dogue
Creek near the old George Washington grist mill.

A copy of Maquilxochitz "Five Flowers," God
of Spring and Flowers, on display in the National
Museum of Natural History. Right: The Fenykovi
elephant, a twelve ton African giant, the largest
land animal of modern times is one of the more
popular exhibits in the museum.

African drums on display in the National Museum of
Natural History. The use of modern display
techniques add immediacy to the exhibit. Right:
Lighted fossil of the *ichthyos aurus* found in Germany.
This represents one of approximately thirteen
million specimens of plant and animal fossils in the
department of paleobiology.

"All the great laws of society are laws of nature."

TOM PAINE

Sculptures depicting the writings of William
Shakespeare line the north wall of the Folger
Shakespeare Library. Right: The symbol of infinity is
utilized by José de Rivera in his sculpture at the
Madison Drive entrance to the National Museum of
History and Technology.

THE TRAGEDIE OF MACBETH

Seated 19 feet above its pedestal, Lincoln faces out through the Ionic columns of the Lincoln Memorial Building. The sculpture designed by artist Daniel Chester French was carved from twenty-eight blocks of Georgia marble. Right: White-blossomed cherry trees line the shores of the Tidal Basin. The stately Jefferson Memorial is in the background.

"Here was a man to hold against the world, a man to
match the mountains and the sea."

EDWIN MARKHAM of Lincoln

Winter's generous mantle covers a path along Dumbarton Oaks estate in Georgetown. Right: General Grant is one of the world's largest equestrian statues. Facing west on the Mall at 1st Street, the Grant Memorial is the most expensive statuary grouping in Washington.

Below and Right: Monuments of bronze and stone enhance the beauty of Theodore Roosevelt Island. It is a part of the National Capital Park System. This 88-acre wilderness preserve in the Potomac River was authorized by Congress in 1932 to honor President Roosevelt's contributions to conservation.

"I hate a man who would skin the land."

THEODORE ROOSEVELT

Tourists, counted in the millions, from every state
in the Union and every nation in the world visit
Washington annually. Right: Guides are ever
helpful in revealing choice bits of information. Here
in a setting of beauty and history one can visualize
America's heritage as nowhere else in the land.

Entrance to Rock Creek Parkway at Watergate. Arlington is in the background across the Potomac River. Right: The great falls of the Potomac is a favorite recreation and picnic area. It is located about nine miles upriver from the capital city.

A visitor reflects quiet solitude below a sculpture in the rotunda of the National Gallery of Art. Over two million visitors a year tour the spacious halls and view its twenty-seven thousand works of art. The gallery is part of the Smithsonian complex. Right: The old Smithsonian building across the Mall, wherein are the headquarters for this enormous program.

Lafayette looking out from the square where it has
been said the nation begins. Right: Rock Creek Park,
largest of our National Capital Parks, covers some
eighteen hundred acres and is unmatched as an
urban wilderness. It was originally acquired in 1890.

Bronze symbol signifying the balance of justice decorates the base of a flag pole at the Supreme Court Building. Right: The building is constructed of Vermont marble, with some of the exterior slabs weighing as much as 63 tons. President Herbert Hoover laid the cornerstone in 1932. Only the Archives and Lincoln Memorial can match the scale and grandeur of its architectural classicism.

"If there is any principle of the constitution that more imperatively
calls for attachment than any other it is the principle of
free thought—not free thought for those who agree with us
but freedom for the thought that we hate."

OLIVER WENDELL HOLMES, JR.

Bartholdi Fountain standing south of Independence Avenue from the Botanic Gardens. The gardens were used originally to house botanical collections of nineteenth century expeditions. Right: Cherry trees in blossom line the Tidal Basin at West Potomac Park.

Visitors seem completely relaxed among the marble
pillars at the Constitution Avenue entrance to the
National Gallery of Art. The gallery maintains a
collection of paintings, sculpture, and graphic arts
dating back to the twelfth century. Right: Eighteenth
century sculpture of Louis XIV, gift from the Kress
collection on display in the west hall.

Building date marker secured to the steps of the
Octagon House denotes its age. Right: Statue of
Alexander Hamilton lends authority to the south
entrance of the Treasury Building. Hamilton pos-
sessed one of the greatest financial and organiza-
tional minds in America.

THE TREASURY DEPARTMENT
ALEXANDER HAMILTON
1757–1804
FIRST SECRETARY OF THE TREASURY
SOLDIER ORATOR STATESMAN
CHAMPION OF CONSTITUTIONAL UNION
REPRESENTATIVE GOVERNMENT AND
NATIONAL INTEGRITY

Expressing formality and elegance, the Pan-American Union is truly one of Washington's most beautiful buildings. Completed in 1910 this white marble structure was designed by Albert Kelsey and Paul Cret. Right: The sky-lighted entrance court houses many rare and treasured tropical plants.

A now extinct Chital deer flees a menacing tiger on display in the National Museum of Natural History in taxidermy by Louis Paul Jonas. Right: The museum, an integral part of the Smithsonian complex, has a collection in excess of fifty million bird and animal specimens both for exhibit and scientific study.

Marine Corps War Memorial reveals in reality the
raising of the colors on Iwo Jima in 1945. Situated
north of Arlington National Cemetery it honors the
men of the U.S. Marine Corps who gave their lives
for their country since the Corps was founded in
1775. Right: An architectural graphic design adorns
National Guard Memorial on Massachusetts Avenue.

"Wherever there is a human being, I see God-given rights inherent in that being, whatever may be the sex or complexion."

WILLIAM LLOYD GARRISON

NATIONAL GUARD
MEMORIAL

Nature symbols of grass and leaves superimposed
over ancient architectural forms and space age
machines dazzle the imagination in a light show
in the Corcoran Gallery of Art. Right: Bronze lion
adjoining the front entrance to this famous gallery
keeps a wary eye out for all visitors.

Bronze sculpture of President Kennedy (height 7 feet) dominates the south wall of the foyer in the John F. Kennedy Center for the Performing Arts. Right: The foyer (length 630 feet) overlooks the Potomac River. Gifts of art and craft objects from many nations provide much of the interior decor.

"I am certain that after the dust of centuries has passed over our cities, we too, will be remembered not for victories or defeats in battle or in politics, but for our contribution to the human spirit."

JOHN F. KENNEDY

Ducks move leisurely along in the old Chesapeake & Ohio Canal close to Lock 20. In background the Great Falls Tavern, now a museum of the National Park Service. Right: A young artist reflects a steady hand at a "Summer in the Park" program in the city.

Life changes in the federal city as town houses are abandoned for the more stylish apartments in the ever-congested Washington. Right: A figure at the base of the James A. Garfield statue depicts the frontiersman, a part of Garfield's career.

View from west side of Capitol Building along the
Mall. In background, three prominent structures
from left to right: the Smithsonian, Washington
Monument and National Gallery of Art. Right: Marble
carving of the head of Lincoln in the Capitol rotunda
below the monumental fresco of the great dome.

"This embryo capital, where fancy sees squares in morasses, obelisks in trees; which second-sighted seers, ev'n now, adorn with shrines unbuilt and heroes yet unborn. Where naught but woods and Jefferson they see, where streets should run and sages ought to be."

THOMAS MOORE—1804

The Arts and Industries Building primarily contains
exhibits of the National Air and Space Museum,
from Kitty Hawk to rockets. Right: Navy and Marine
Memorial to the men who died at sea, located in
Lady Bird Johnson Park on the Potomac.

Still reflecting beauty from the past, this cluster of
homes awaits its fate, be it renovation or doom.
Right: Young man cultivates his own garden in the
National Arboretum. This youth garden program in
Washington is conducted through the Department
of Recreation for the District of Columbia.

The mansion at Mt. Vernon from the main gate. The last additions by George Washington were completed in 1787. Right: A tasteful brick fence divides the stable yard from the kitchen garden, restored in a style true to the manner of Washington's era.

Mt. Vernon landing on the Potomac River. Constructed now of contemporary materials, the landing was once the supply and shipping point for the plantation. Right: Fences border the botanical garden that was used by George Washington for experimental planting at Mt. Vernon.

Neighborhood teenagers frolic on the equestrian
statue of General George Washington in Washington
Circle. Right: Young naturalist scales snowy hillside
in Montrose Park. Beautiful in any season, it is
adjacent to Dumbarton Oaks and Rock Creek Parks.

"One man outweighs them all in influence over the people."

THOMAS JEFFERSON of George Washington

An aircraft comes in over the colonnaded Jefferson Memorial en route to the Washington National Airport. Right: Elegant gilded statue in Judiciary Square erected in honor of Joseph Darlington, 1849-1920, counselor, teacher and lover of mankind.

The Adams Memorial, masterful sculpture by
Augustus Saint Gaudens, nestled in a holly grove in
Rock Creek Cemetery. Right: Rock Creek spills
over a dam at Pierce Mill. This creek is one of the
significant natural features within the city.

"The interest of the figure was not in its meaning,
but in the response of the observer."

HENRY ADAMS

A reproduction of Hindu-Javanese wood carving adorning a shop wall in Georgetown offers a little respite from the great monuments that dot the city. Right: Fall delivers an exciting splash of color in the garden of the Japanese Embassy.

Not only Americans, but visitors and representatives
of diplomatic services from all over the world, view
the splendors of Washington. Right: Monument
recalls the heroics of Major General Philip Kearny
of New Jersey in Arlington National Cemetery.

"Only admit the original, unalterable truth, that all men are
equal in their rights, and the foundation of everything is laid."

JOEL BARLOW

The auditorium in the Interstate Commerce Commission Building, on Constitution Avenue, typifies the federal triangle complex. Though constructed independently, the buildings were conceived as a single monumental unit. This bureaucratic quarter was built in the decade 1928-1938. Right: White cherry blossoms offer unusual contrast against the west side of the veiled Capitol dome.

A city of people, parks and pigeons is reflected under the noon shade of elms in LaFayette Park. Right: Fountain dedicated to the memory of Oscar S. Straus, author and diplomat, for serving his country with distinction in high office from 1887 to 1926. Located in the court north of the Department of Labor.

"The voice of reason is more to be regarded than the bent of any present inclination."

OSCAR S. STRAUS

141

Fountain inside the driveway of the Smithsonian's National Museum of History and Technology illustrates some of the beauty of night time Washington. Right: Dress Dolley Madison wore at a reception in the White House in 1816 on display in this museum. The museum preserves and displays outstanding treasures of the American people.

Interior beauty of the Library of Congress is intensi-
fied by mosaics, statues and archways of carved
marble. Among its priceless treasures are the Guten-
berg Bible and the Gettysburg address in the hand
of Lincoln. Right: Camera captures the delicate
craftsmanship and design of ceiling and arch.

"—There is, in fact, no subject to which a member of congress
may not have occasion to refer."

THOMAS JEFFERSON

Sea-nymph triumphantly bestriding an infuriated
sea horse, a part of the fountain by Hinton Perry in
front of the Library of Congress. Right: View from
the visitor's gallery in the library, the dome of the
main reading room, may well leave even the most
sophisticated a little numb.

The German Embassy Chancery, with its glass and
steel structure, offers one of Washington's outstanding examples of contemporary architecture. It
is situated on Reservoir Road, Northwest. Right:
Rock Creek flows softly through the city before
entering the Potomac.

Simon Bolivar, the liberator, reflecting the glory
that was his, stands on a street island adjacent to
the Interior Department on Virginia Avenue. Right:
Authentic tea house in the garden of the Japanese
Embassy sprinkled with autumn leaves.

An early morning jogger makes his way up the steps to the great doric colonnade of the Lincoln Memorial. Visitors come at all hours to give homage to the man, Lincoln. Even though a borrowed Greek temple form, the memorial attains a nobility which transcends its eclectic heritage. Right: Brilliant color spectacle greets late evening visitors.

"With malice toward none, with charity for all, with
firmness in the right as God gives us to see right."

ABRAHAM LINCOLN

Frantic horses draw a cannon within the Grant
Memorial in Union Square. This statuary grouping,
some 252 feet in length, was completed in the
1920's by artist Henry Shrady. Right: Furled flags
surrounding the Washington Monument say aloud,
"Old Glory, the symbol of liberty."

154

"There must be no second class citizens in this country."

DWIGHT D. EISENHOWER

Tomb of the unknown soldier, a hallowed place of remembrance, is guarded 24 hours a day. Right: Arlington National Cemetery, a final resting place for America's honored dead, the known and the unknown, the great and the humble.

Letter forms add eye appeal to the windows of grocery store in Chinatown. Right: Center of DuPont Circle is anchored by this delightful fountain. It is a memorial to Rear Admiral Samuel F. DuPont, a Civil War naval hero, for whom the circle was named. It was created by Daniel Chester French.

Fiery ball of the setting sun dominates the horizon as commuters wend their way homeward over the Arlington Bridge. Right: The unique Scaley Gate at the entrance to Arlington National Cemetery, a cherished shrine dating back to its founding in 1864.

"The true honor of a nation is to be found only
in deeds of justice, and in the happiness of its people,
all of which are inconsistent with war."

CHARLES SUMNER

Spectator admiring the statue at the Lincoln Memorial in early morning. Right: The Spiral created by Alexander Calder, rests in the courtyard of the National Collection of Fine Arts. A benefaction of the artist, it was completed in 1966.

"—and that government of the people, by the people, for the people, shall not perish from the earth."

ABRAHAM LINCOLN

Viewed through an archway of the new Post Office
Department Building, the clock tower of the old
Post Office reflects the architectural styling of 1899.
Right: Visitors walk amidst the ring of flags under
the great national memorial to George Washington.
Begun in 1833 and after many difficulties and delays
this marble shaft 555 feet 5⅛ inches in height was
completed and opened to the public in 1888.

Bird enclosure designed for maximum freedom in flight at the National Zoological Park. Visitors may enter and walk among the birds. Right: Detail from the German contribution to the John F. Kennedy Center. It consists of two bronze reliefs placed near the main entrance; each over 40 feet long with themes of "America" and "War or Peace."

"Our most dangerous tendency is to expect too much of government, and at the same time do for it too little."

WARREN G. HARDING

Thomas Jefferson Memorial erected along the south banks of Washington's Tidal Basin, designed in a style Jefferson admired. The colonnaded structure sits on a line with the south axis of the White House. This location is not only aesthetic but befitting the importance of Jefferson in the nation's history. Right: Visitors seem minute in relation to massive columns of the Memorial. In background the Washington Monument juts skyward to dominate the horizon.

Early mode of luxurious transportation. The Concord Coach was built in 1880 for the run between Williamsville and East Dover, Vermont. Right: Excellent example of wood carving from a turn-of-the-century circus vehicle on display at the National Museum of History and Technology.

Famous Yoshino cherry trees give the Tidal Basin
a brilliant splash of color in early spring. Right: A jet
lowers its flaps en route to the Washington National
Airport, one of the world's busiest terminals. Aircraft
arrive and depart at seemingly one minute intervals.

"The heritage of the past is the seed that brings forth
the harvest of the future."

NATIONAL ARCHIVES

Ducks express no fear in Roaches Run Waterfowl
Sanctuary. It is located on the Virginia side of the
Potomac River across from East Potomac Park. Right:
Boats moored in the Boundary Channel Lagoon
reflect a life of leisure. In background, the Pentagon.

Tobacco fields flourish along the Patuxent River, near Washington where in this vicinity the British landed in 1814 to invade and burn the young city. Right: Cannon in old Fort Marcey, a Civil War entrenchment up the Potomac from the capital city.

"I was not born to acknowledge a master."

ALEXANDER H. STEPHENS, constitutionalist

The Federal Trade Commission Building forms the
apex of the federal triangle, extending westward from
Constitution and Pennsylvania Avenues. Right:
Detail of one of the 14-foot high statues outside the
Commission Building symbolizes trade control. The
statues were a W.P.A. project commissioned in 1938.

"The constitution of the United States was made not merely for
the generation that then existed, but for posterity—"

HENRY CLAY

Sign of spring on the Potomac. Fishermen troll the river below the Palisades. Right: Massive and well proportioned contemporary sculpture on exhibit in L'Enfant Plaza dominates the human scale.

Plaster cast of the face of Abraham Lincoln by
Leonard Volk in 1860. It is on display at Ford's Theatre
Museum, 511 Tenth Street Northwest. Right: Statue
of Chief Justice John Marshall posed as a supreme
jurist rendering a decision. Unveiled in 1884 on the
west plaza of the Capitol.

"The law, wherein, as in a magic mirror, we see reflected not only
our own lives, but the lives of all men that have been."

OLIVER WENDELL HOLMES, JR